EVERYTHING I
NEED TO KNOW
I LEARNED FROM
MY DOG

by Richard Smith

Illustrated by Debra Solomon

Sterling Publishing Co., Inc.
New York

A John Boswell Associates Book

Design by Nan Jernigan

Library of Congress
Cataloging-in-Publication Data Available

2 4 6 8 10 9 7 5 3 1

Published by Sterling Publishing Co., Inc.
387 Park Avenue South, New York, NY 10016
© 2006 by Sterling Publishing Co., Inc.

Distributed in Canada by Sterling Publishing
c/o Canadian Manda Group, 165 Dufferin Street
Toronto, Ontario, Canada M6K 3H6
Distributed in the United Kingdom by
GMC Distribution Services
Castle Place, 166 High Street, Lewes, East Sussex,
England BN7 1XU
Distributed in Australia by Capricorn Link (Australia) Pty. Ltd.
P.O. Box 704, Windsor, NSW 2756, Australia

Sterling ISBN-13: 978-1-4027-4236-1
ISBN-10: 1-4027-4236-3

For information about custom editions, special
sales, premium and corporate purchases, please contact
Sterling Special Sales Department at 800-805-5489
or specialsales@sterlingpub.com.

Everything I Need to Know I Learned From My Dog

 If dogs could speak, and I'm not saying they don't, what might they tell us? Unlike cats, who really don't know very much, the average dog is wise beyond its years, articulate with its tail, discerning with its nose, generous with a smile (if it likes your jokes[1]) and overwhelmingly affectionate with its tongue, especially if your hand happens to be holding a lamb chop. All they ask in return is that you feed them, pet them, give them room when they vigorously wag their tails and, above all, keep them away from dog groomers who insist they'd look better in bangs.

 A dog's "sixth sense" somehow lets you know that you look fantastic in that clingy knit dress (and without sucking in). If you've had a bad day, a dog sits patiently as you wipe away your tears with its tail. Dogs make wonderful outdoor companions: on a picnic, a dog's barking will repel even the most determined ants, it will chase away assertive crows and, if it's windy, sit and hold one end of the blanket down. And, best of all, I've yet to meet the dog who obeys a NO PETS ALLOWED sign. I have learned much from dogs, I hope you will, too.

---

[1]Dogs have a sense of humor. Cats, alas, are pretty much humorless.

• *Love is blind.*

- Don't be afraid to explore.

- Get a good eighteen hours of sleep a day.

- Make people feel welcome, even if they've only been gone for thirty seconds.

Sex without love is meaningless.

Being a Dog Means

1. Being able to wear the same outfit every day.

2. Dinner hour is never interrupted by a telemarketer.

3. The IRS can't touch you.

4. You don't need a passport.

5. Your kids will never blame you for how they turned out.

* *You can burst into song whenever you feel like it.*

7

Six Ways to Make Your Dog Really Happy

1. Tell your guests to leave and let him have the run of the Thanksgiving table.

2. Hold each other close while watching *Singin' in the Rain*.

3. Torture the cat.

4. Include his face, too, when you put your photo on Match.Com.

5. Dim the lights and slow-dance to the music of Glenn Miller. (Make sure the shades are pulled.)

6. Point out how the new collar you bought makes her look five pounds lighter.

Little things mean a lot.

- Never be embarrassed by public displays of affection.

- Never try to race across a waxed hard wood floor.

- When all else fails, nap.

It's important to pursue your dreams.

Puppy Love Pop Quiz #1

True or False

You love your dog if:

Two or more photos of doggie are in your wallet or camera phone.
T___ F___

She's in your will.
T___ F___

You have a special voice that you use only with her.
T___ F___

In the privacy of your home, you've danced together.
T___ F___

You're really addressing the dog when you call out, "Honey, I'm home."
T___ F___

Your carry-on luggage includes your dog
T___ F___

At night, when she kicks you out of bed and tells you to go in the other room because you snore, you obey.
T___ F___

You break out the good china on her birthday.
T___ F___

Scoring: If you answered "true" to every question, it's possible that your dog owns you.

- *One lick is worth a hundred antidepressants.*

- It's nice to feel pampered.

- It's okay to indulge once in a while.

- A little praise goes a long way.

● *Holding for the next customer*
  service rep doesn't have to be
  a lonely event.

16

For Old Dogs

1. It's easier to lie about your age.

2. You can reach your target heart rate by wagging your tail.

3. You don't have to worry about not making it to the bathroom.

4. Your retirement is fully funded.

5. No matter where you doze off, you're excused.

6. You can get away with forgetting birthdays.

• You can't give someone too many pats on the head.

> *"I'm not spoiled, but when it comes to chewing, I much prefer expensive Italian loafers to dried up slippers."*
>
> —*Cedrick*, the finicky poodle

- A fool and his meatloaf are soon parted.

- Scotchguard is a great invention.

• Cats are overrated.

BEING A DOG MEANS

1. Automatically taking a vow of poverty.

2. Not caring if your new doll is anatomically correct.

3. You don't have to pass solid geometry.

4. Your personal assistant is always on duty.

5. When you find yourself attracted to another dog, you don't worry, "Is he gay?"

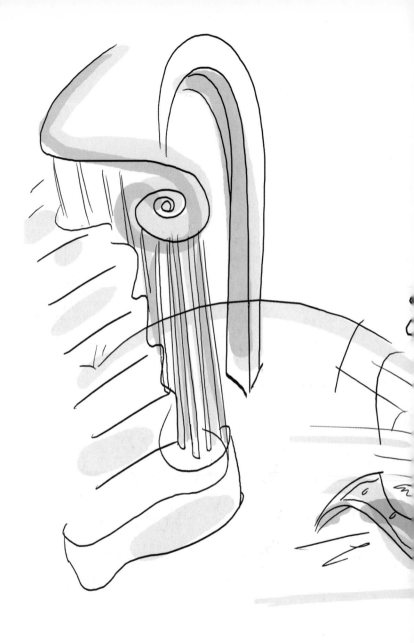

Look before you leap.

It's a Dog's Life

1. Every day is a day off.

2. You always know where your next meal is coming from.

3. The world is full of toys.

4. Eating like a slob is expected of you . . . and even kind of cute.

• Being a pet has its advantages.

Be flexible.

GREAT MOMENTS IN DOGDOM

ACTUAL QUOTES FROM ACTUAL DOGS:

*"My enthusiasm for retrieving thrown
sticks is intensified when they're made of
pepperoni."*
> —*Benito*, the Yorkie who is easily
> bribed with meat products

*"It's traumatic when I chase a squirrel
who suddenly turns around and starts
chasing me. What's up with that?*
> —*Clyde*, the sissy rottweiler

*"If you feel something go bump in the
night, not to worry. I'm merely trying to
bury my bone in the mattress."*
> —*Hermann*, the psychotic pug

"Obedience training is for owners."
> —*Balto*, assistant lead
> husky and anarchist

• *Don't panic if you oversleep.*

- Be resourceful.

- Be inquisitive.

- Be assertive.

• Be **BOLD.**

29

Things a Dog Needn't Worry About

- Finding a bathing suit that fits.

- Water retention.

- Gaining weight during the holiday season.

- Sun-damaged skin.

- Cellulite.

- Wearing the pants in the family.

Always have your getaway planned.

Excerpts from
My Dog's Little Instruction Book

What I Really Think

- When you say, "Bad dog," I pretend to feel remorse, but I don't.

- I terrorize only those guests who deserve it.

- Telling me to fetch is demeaning.

- Only a chump leaves the Thanksgiving turkey where I can get at it.

Speaking My Language

- Shedding is my way of expressing love.

- When I sit by the door vigorously wagging my tail, it means either
    1) I'm desperate to go out, or
    2) An insurance salesman is about to call.

- Would it kill you to occasionally bark at me? It's nice to hear my own language.

Excerpts from
My Dog's Little Instruction Book

Bathroom Etiquette

- Saying, "Good boy," after I do my business does not increase my self-esteem.

- When you "pick up after me," please don't let me see it.

- Be patient if I'm sniffing out the perfect spot to make. When it comes to public restrooms, I'm fussy.

- Stop examining my poop. It's embarrassing.

Good Advice

- Give people more than they expect. This applies especially to me when I'm begging for table scraps.

- Never wear pearls when giving me a bath.

- When you speak to me, talk slowly. English is a difficult language.

• *Never take no for an answer.*

• *We all put on a few extra pounds during the holidays.*

BEING A DOG MEANS

1. Someone else pays when I chew through my leash.

2. Someone else cleans up the mud you track into the house.

3. Crow's feet are edible.

4. Looking extra cute cancels out "Bad dog!"

- *Comfort food doesn't have to be fattening.*

• It's wise to lick the hand that feeds you.

• It's acceptable to yawn when guests bore you.

• When all else fails, look sheepish.

Looks are everything.

Family Planning

Which Dogs Make the Best Sleeping Companions?

Slumber tests by Consumer Reports found very few breeds who were able to meet the exacting standard of "sleeping companion" as set forth by PETA in their recent "Dogs With Least Offensive Morning Breath" position paper. We present the results below:

Breed Traits

Collie
A model dog-citizen and wonderful source of warmth without weight. Delighted to lie quietly beside you while you read a trashy novel, then tenderly kiss you good night before you doze off. A real animal in bed.

Chihuahua
Cuddly but high strung, plus those bulgy eyes glow in the dark. Negative reaction to designer sheets may prompt discovery of tiny pellets induced by what dog psychiatrists term "inappropriate relaxation."

Doberman
Very protective, very territorial but lots of empathy—can sense when owner is having a bad dream and will gently blow in distressed owner's ear until dream improves.

Akita
Faithful, loving and born hibernators. Alas, if not given their fair share of the covers, they wet the bed.

Bloodhound
Very calm, very thoughtful. The canine of choice for finding lost earrings, scrunchies and the convict hiding in your basement at 3 a.m.

Golden Retriever
Adorably furry and good natured, with an exquisite sense of smell—if doorbell rings, can differentiate between a tot selling Girl Scout cookies and a Jehovah's Witness, allowing owner to either open the door or hide beneath the covers. It may occasionally bring a still-quacking duck to bed.

Toy Terrier

Easy to sneak past a co-op board, loves being rocked to sleep. Can be used as your pillow in an emergency. Because of its tiny bladder, however, it may get up six times a night to pee.

Bichon Frise

A marvelous companion if owner in bed with the flu. Will happily lick face and commiserate until either you're better or drown. Will even hold phone so you can call in sick without straining. Mixture of French-Belgian makes them impulsive squirrel chasers—bad if you sleep with the window open and the bed is next to a branch.

Mutt

Loving and devoted, especially if rescued from a mean dog pound. Compulsive do-gooders, may appear at the foot of your bed holding a rodent in its teeth, wearing a "Who's the best doggie in the world?" expression.

Newfoundland

The best. Not only are they among the most soft-hearted of dogs, they're fluffy, fun to cuddle and certain to keep your feet warm on frosty nights. They love when you read them a bedtime story, preferably Little Red Riding Hood (they like to identify with the wolf).

German Shepherd

A fabulous sleeping companion (receiver of the coveted 2006 Restful Night's Sleep award from the ASPCA). Will cling extra-close if it senses you need warmth and, if you're having trouble dozing off, will croon a soothing lullaby in your ear. Best of all, a shepherd is low maintenance: he'll gladly make his own breakfast if you leave the refrigerator door open.

• *Persistence is everything.*

> *"I'm perplexed. My owner keeps tossing the ball, I retrieve it, he hurls it again, I retrieve it. What am I missing, doesn't he want it?*
>
> —*Sid*, the baffled terrier

- Never yell "Fire hydrant!" in a crowded dog park.

- Keep your paws out of the wall sockets.

- *It's not the gift, it's the thought that counts.*

SIX MORE WAYS TO MAKE YOUR DOG REALLY HAPPY

1. Praise her when she bites the mailman because he brought you only bills.

2. If she's sensitive, don't let her know that her barking all night disturbs the neighbors.

3. Before throwing it, marinate her ball in chopped liver.

4. When grocery shopping, let her ride in the cart.

5. If she forgets where she buried her bone, help her. (Metal detectors with a "find doggie's bone" setting are available online.)

6. Tell her, "Good dog," if she gets detention in dog obedience class.

Puppy Love Pop Quiz #2

True or False

You love your dog if:

1. You ask, "What kind of topping would you like, boy?" before ordering your pizza.
    T___ F___

2. You shower him with praise when he chews up your slipper.
    T___ F___

3. His pleading eyes induce you to give him the "doggie bag" containing half your $100 meal.
    T___ F___

4. Saying, "Gooooooooooood boy," makes you feel better than your dog.
    T___ F___

5. No matter how hard it's raining, if he has to go out, you take him, instead of just holding him out the window and shaking.
T___ F___

6. The photo of doggie you keep in your wallet is life size.
T___ F___

7. When he sits on your lap while you're driving, you sometimes, in light traffic, let him:
   a) steer. T___ F___
   b) play with the directional signals. T___ F___

8. You wouldn't think of using her tail as a potholder.
T___ F___

Scoring: If you answered true to all eight questions, seek counseling.

• *A bubble bath is the perfect way to spend a romantic evening.*

52

Being a Dog Means

Five things you'll never get stressed over:

1. That first gray hair

2. Love handles

3. Jury duty

4. Putting your puppies through college

5. Accidentally drooling on a guest's knee

• *Your reach should exceed your grasp.*

- When holding a bake sale, don't ask your dog to help.

- Shake hands like you mean it.

- The neighbors will never know who stole their newspaper.

Letting the world go to the dogs. . .

may not be such a bad thing.

• *Be cool if you're abducted by aliens.*

- You *can* face the world without coffee.

- Walking is a great way to reduce stress.

- Sometimes a cookie can make all the difference.

• *Be master of all you survey.*

• Always keep your resume current.

RESUME

Name: Rover

Puppyhood ambition: Find a good home

Fondest memory: My first bone

Wildest dream: Retrieve waterfowl for my master.

Second wildest dream: Eat them

Proudest moment: Leading a protest against *Cats*.

Biggest challenge: Convincing my owner that three daily servings of sirloin steak are good for my fur

Perfect day: Sleeping late

Perfect night: Taunting the cat

First job: Watch dog, used car lot

Current position: Drug-sniffing dog, DEA

Indulgences:

  1. Collecting signed photos of famous dogs.

  2. My three Gucci leashes

Favorite movies: 1. *Finding Nemo* 2. *Quo Vadis* 3. *Lassie versus Godzilla*

Inspirations: Lassie, Balto and Mother Teresa

Hobbies: Dozing, sleeping and logarithms

• *Always stretch before undertaking physical activity.*

• *Eat your vegetables.*

- Begging is a useful skill.

- Utensils are pretentious.

- "Woof woof" is a great pickup line.

Catnaps aren't limited to cats.

Leave the heavy lifting to your inferiors.

Being a Dog Means

1. You'll never, ever go bald.

2. The TV remote is edible.

3. Never worrying, "Where's the nearest bathroom?"

4. Fur is a surprisingly affordable way to keep warm.

• *Make a habit of good personal hygiene.*

• One bark is worth a thousand words.

• Take pride in your appearance.

• Unconditional love makes the world brighter.

- *A bad hair day is not the end of the world.*

• *It's nice to wake up next to someone you love.*

PAT: Pet Assessment Test

How Much Does Your Doggie Know?

(Please check all that apply.)

Bites suspicious strangers ___

Steals neighbor's newspaper ___

Catches a Frisbee ___

Rolls over and plays:
    dead ___
    in the mud ___

Wipes paws before coming inside ___

Sleeps ___

Begs ___

Fetches ___

Barks at the mailman ___

Heels ___

Attacks your ex ___

Discreetly poops on hateful neighbor's lawn ___

Has stopped licking TV screen during cooking shows ___

Comes when called ___

Obeys commands:
    "Get away from that pot roast!" ___
    "Put the cat down!" ___

Growls if the plumber overcharges ___

- If you hang around a table long enough, something good will happen.

- There is no such thing as junk food portion control.

- The way to a loved one's heart is through his stomach.

Beg and ye shall receive.

- *Make sure you're dressed when you ask, "Do you want to go out?"*

- "The dog ate my spreadsheet" *is* a viable excuse.

- "I'll just have a taste" is for sissies.

- "Do you want to go out?" is a trick question.

• *First impressions count.*

> **"I hate my name."**
> —*Ethel*, the golden retriever
> (and love child of Mordecai
> and Mabel)

- Choose names with care (that applies to pets *and* children).

- Mental health is a state of mind.

• *Puppy love is sometimes better than the real thing.*

Wind-blown is a good look.

• *Size isn't important.*

• Never park by a fire hydrant.

• Make vigorous exercise part of your routine.

• The smaller the creature, the bigger the ego.

• *Bottled water is a waste of money.*

BEING A DOG MEANS

Fluency in any language:

Greetings in Italian: "Arf"
Greetings in Finnish: "Arf"
Greetings in Dutch: "Arf"
Greetings in Korean: "Arf"
Greetings in Arabic: "Arf"
Greetings in Polish: "Arf"
Greetings in Swahili: "Arf"

One wag is worth a thousand words.

- It's never too late to have a happy puppyhood!